Ketogenic Diet for Beginners:
A Diet of Low Carb Recipes for Weight Loss

Free Gift Included

As part of our commitment to making sure you live a healthy lifestyle, we have included a free e-book in the link below. This book looks at improving every aspect of your life in the long term; including diet, sleep and exercise. I hope that you enjoy this e-book and the extra gift as well. The link to the gift is below:

http://36potentfoodstoloseweightandlivehealthy.gr8.com

Disclaimer

Copyright © 2016

All Rights Reserved.

No part of this eBook can be transmitted or reproduced in any form including print, electronic, photocopying, scanning, mechanical or recording without prior written permission from the author.

While the author has taken utmost efforts to ensure the accuracy of the written content, all readers are advised to follow information mentioned herein at their own risk. The author cannot be held responsible for any personal or commercial damage caused by information. All readers are encouraged to seek professional advice when needed.

Book description

This book is a guide for all those who want to follow the Ketogenic Diet, but have no clue where to begin. It contains detailed information as to what the Ketogenic Diet is, the do's and don'ts of the diet and a bunch of recipes that will help you kick-start your journey!

This book is full of Ketogenic Diet-friendly recipes for a variety of meals, such as soups, salads, side dishes, main courses, Ketogenic snacks and last, but not least, desserts!

All the recipes in this book are quick and easy to prepare and you will not need to spend hours in the kitchen. All the ingredients in the recipes are easily available and you do not need to go hunting for expensive specialized ingredients!

With this bunch of Ketogenic Diet-friendly recipes, you can easily and quickly pick up the diet without having to do any calorie calculations or gram-by-gram portion measurements!

This book is one stop for all your Ketogenic Diet queries!

Table of Contents

Free Gift Included 2

Disclaimer 3

Book description 4

Table of Contents 6

Introduction 11

Ketogenic Breakfast Recipes 15

    Spicy Shrimp Omelet 15

    Raspberry Pancakes 16

    Mock McGriddle Casserole 17

    Meat Bagel 19

    Breakfast Cereal Mix 20

    Avocado Breakfast Bowl 21

    Skillet-Baked Eggs 22

    Cheese Muffins 24

    Chocolate Smoothie 25

Green Smoothie 26

Berry Chocolate Shake 27

Matcha Smoothie Bowl 28

Healthy Smoothie 29

Ketogenic Soup Recipes 30

Chicken Enchilada Soup 30

Spanish Sardine and Tomato Soup 31

Hot Chili Soup 33

Chilled Avocado Soup 35

Light Zucchini Soup 36

Cream of Broccoli Soup 37

Cream of Mushroom Soup 38

Ketogenic Salad Recipes 40

Tuna Salad 40

Cold Chicken Salad 40

Egg and Avocado Salad 42

Tri Color Salad 43

Caper and Lemon Salad 44

Salmon, Bacon and Kale Salad 45

Thai Salad 46

Ketogenic Main Course Recipes 48

Spicy Chicken Nuggets 48

Chicken in Butter Gravy 49

Ground Pork Tacos 51

Italian Pork Cutlets 52

Sri Lankan Fish Curry 53

Coconut and Shrimp Avocadoes 55

Baked Salmon 56

Lamb Souvlaki (Greek Lamb Skewers) 58

Ground Beef and Spinach Skillet 59

Low-Carb Shepherd's Pie 60

Spinach Pie 62

Low-Carb Pad Thai 63

Stir Fried Bacon & Vegetables 64

- Zucchini Casserole 65
- Low-Carb Pizza 66

Ketogenic Side Dishes 68
- Cauliflower Garlic Breadsticks 68
- Keto Bread / Muffins 69
- Mashed Cauliflower (Mock Mashed Potatoes) 70
- Mushroom and Hemp Seeds Pilaf 71
- Cauliflower Rice 72

Ketogenic Snack Recipes 74
- Healthy Granola Bars 74
- Fish Fingers 75
- Fried Cheese Sticks 76
- Pizza Bites 77

Ketogenic Dessert Recipes 79
- Raspberry Chia Pudding 79
- Berry Ice Cream 80
- Strawberry Cheesecake 81

Chocolate and Peanut Butter Bites 82

Conclusion 83

Introduction

In a world obsessed with size zero, it seems every person with an ounce of extra weight wants to lose it. Capitalizing on this trend, a lot of "dieticians" and "nutritionists" have come up with a variety of "specialized diets" where you consume "special foods" and lose weight. All this is just a sham!

The reality is that most of the time, these "specialists" have deals with manufacturing companies, and they push the "special" products produced by companies in your face to earn a hefty commission. At the end of these diets all you will have lost is money! But, what if I tell you that there is a diet in which you do not need to purchase expensive specialized products (nor starve) and you can still lose weight without messing up your regular schedule?

Here I present to you the "**Ketogenic Diet**".

The Ketogenic Diet is quite popular, as it is a low-carb diet. The body usually converts carbohydrates to glucose and insulin. Glucose is the most basic and easiest energy source the body can break down and use to provide energy. This is why your body will ignore all sources of energy as long as there is glucose in your system. This results in deposits of fat in the body, because your body stores all the fat from your food for future use.

So, the basic idea of the Ketogenic Diet is to induce the body into a state of *ketosis* by eliminating all carbohydrate-rich foods from the diet. Ketosis is the natural state of the body where the body initiates metabolic processes to deal with the low intake of carbohydrates (and glucose). The body starts producing ketones in the liver by breaking down fat in the body.

While following the Ketogenic Diet, you stop all carbohydrate intake and up your fat intake, resulting in the production of fat-breaking ketones! This breakdown of body fat results in a leaner body!

To start following the Ketogenic Diet, you need to plan ahead and have a diet plan waiting on hand. Whatever you eat has a great impact on how fast your body attains the state of *ketosis*. The lower the carbs that you consume in a day (**preferably less than 15 grams**) the faster your body attains the state of ketosis and the quicker you will lose weight!

Your nutrient intake should be as follows:

- 70% of total nutritional content should be fat
- 25% of total nutritional content should be protein

- 5% of total nutritional content should be carbohydrates

The 5% of carbs should come mostly from dairy, nuts and vegetables, and refined carbs from cereals such as wheat, fruits or starchy vegetables such as potatoes, should be avoided.

An ideal meal should consist of a main protein meal with two sides – one full of veggies and one fat-rich. For example, a meal could consist of a grilled rib-eye steak with a knob of butter and a side of spinach stir fried in olive oil or a whole skinless and boneless chicken breast fried in very little olive oil with a side of stir fried broccoli and cheese.

So, as you can see, this diet aids in the reduction of body fat and helps you to lose weight.

This book contains healthy Ketogenic recipes for all of your meals, from breakfast till dinner and for all courses, from soups to salads to main courses to snacks and desserts! And the best part? All of these recipes are quick and easy and use ingredients easily available in every kitchen and pantry!

I would like to thank you for purchasing this book and I hope you find the content of this book helpful!

Ketogenic Breakfast Recipes

Spicy Shrimp Omelet

Prep: 10 min	Total: 20 min	Servings: 2

Ingredients:

- 3 eggs, whisked
- 2 grape tomatoes, halved
- 1 medium onion, chopped
- 5 shrimp, peeled, deveined
- 1 tablespoon fresh parsley, chopped
- 1/4 teaspoon cayenne pepper
- 1/8 teaspoon pepper powder
- 1/4 teaspoon salt or to taste
- 1 tablespoon coconut oil
- A dash of hot sauce

Method:

1. Place a nonstick pan over medium heat. Add oil. When the oil is hot enough, add onions and sauté until onions are translucent.

2. Add salt, pepper, cayenne pepper, shrimp and tomatoes. Sauté for a couple of minutes.
3. Pour whisked eggs over it. Sprinkle parsley. Cook until the eggs are set.
4. Drizzle hot sauce over it and serve.

Raspberry Pancakes

Prep: 10 min	Total: 25 min	Servings: 2

Ingredients:

- 1 banana, mashed
- 1/2 cup egg whites, beaten
- 6 tablespoons almond milk
- 1 1/2 cup raspberries, frozen
- 1 tablespoon cinnamon
- 2 tablespoons chia seeds, ground
- 2 scoops whey powder
- Cooking spray with olive oil
- 4 tablespoons Greek yogurt to serve

Method:

1. Mix together all the ingredients, except raspberries, until well-combined.
2. Add raspberries and mix again.
3. Place a nonstick pan over medium heat. Spray with olive oil.
4. Pour about 1/4 cup mixture in the pan. Swirl the pan so that the batter spreads. Cook until the bottom side is golden brown.
5. Flip sides. Cook the other side until golden brown.
6. Repeat steps 4 and 5 with the remaining batter.
7. Serve hot with Greek yogurt.

Mock McGriddle Casserole

Prep: 10	Total: 1 hr. 10 min	Servings: 4

Ingredients:

- 5 large eggs
- 2 tablespoons butter
- 1/2-pound breakfast sausages
- 3 tablespoons maple syrup or to taste

- 1/2 teaspoon garlic powder
- 1 teaspoon onion powder
- 2 ounces' cheddar cheese
- 2 tablespoons flaxseed meal
- 1/2 cup almond flour
- Salt to taste
- Pepper powder to taste
- 1/4 teaspoon sage

Method:

1. Place a pan over medium heat. Add sausages and cook until brown and slightly crispy. Remove from heat.
2. Meanwhile, mix together in a large bowl, almond flour, flaxseed meal, salt, pepper, sage, onion and garlic powder.
3. Mix together in another bowl, 2 tablespoons maple syrup and eggs and whisk well. Pour this mixture into the almond flour mixture.
4. Add cheese and stir.
5. Pour this mixture into the pan of sausages and stir. Transfer into a lined casserole dish.
6. Drizzle the remaining tablespoon of maple syrup over it.
7. Place in a preheated oven and bake at 350°F for about 45 minutes or until cooked. A toothpick

when inserted in the center should come out clean.
8. Remove from the oven and cool. Chop into wedges and serve.

Meat Bagel

Prep: 5 min	Total: 55 min	Servings: 4

Ingredients:

- 1-pound ground pork
- 1 medium onion, finely chopped
- 1 large egg
- 1/3 cup tomato sauce
- 1/2 tablespoon butter or ghee
- 1/2 teaspoon paprika
- 1/4 teaspoon pepper powder
- 1/2 teaspoon salt
- Toppings of your choice

Method:

1. Place a skillet over medium heat. Add ghee or butter. When it melts, add onions and sauté until translucent. Remove from heat and cool completely.

2. Transfer into a bowl and add rest of the ingredients and mix well.
3. Divide into 3 or 4 equal portions and shape into a bagel.
4. Place in a baking dish that is lined with parchment paper.
5. Bake in a preheated oven at 400°F for about 40 minutes or until done.
6. Slice the bagels. Fill with toppings of your choice and serve.

Breakfast Cereal Mix

Prep: 5 min	Total: 10 min	Servings: 4

Ingredients:

- 10 tablespoons coconut flakes, unsweetened
- 14 tablespoons hemp seeds
- 10 tablespoons flaxseed, ground
- 4 tablespoons sesame, ground (grind for just a few seconds)
- 4 tablespoons dark cocoa, unsweetened
- 4 tablespoons psyllium husk
- 1 cup almonds, chopped

Method:

1. Mix together all the ingredients and place in an airtight container. Refrigerate until use.
2. To serve, add water or coffee or any non-dairy milk, soak for a while and serve.

Avocado Breakfast Bowl

Prep: 5 min	Total: 5 min	Servings: 4

Ingredients:

- 2 large avocadoes, peeled, pitted, halved
- 4 tablespoons tahini
- 1 large carrot, shredded

For dressing:
- 2 tablespoons lemon juice
- 2 tablespoons extra virgin olive oil
- 1/2 teaspoons ginger, grated
- 1/2 tablespoons poppy seeds
- 1/8 teaspoon salt

Method:

1. Whisk together all the ingredients of the dressing and carrots.
2. Fill the avocado halves with mixture.
3. Top with tahini and serve.
4. Scoop along with the avocado and eat.

Skillet-Baked Eggs

| Prep: 10 min | Total: 40 min | Servings: 6 |

Ingredients:

- 1 cup plain Greek yogurt
- 2 cloves garlic, halved
- Kosher salt to taste
- 3 tablespoons unsalted butter, divided
- 3 tablespoons olive oil
- 5 tablespoons leek, chopped, white and pale green part only

- 3 tablespoons scallions, chopped, white and pale green parts only
- 15 ounces' fresh spinach, rinsed
- 2 teaspoons fresh lemon juice
- 6 large eggs
- 1/2 teaspoon crushed red pepper flakes
- 1/4 teaspoon paprika
- 2 teaspoons fresh oregano, chopped

Method:

1. To a small bowl, add yogurt, garlic and a pinch of salt. Mix well and keep aside.
2. Place a skillet over medium heat. Add half the butter. When butter melts, add leeks and scallions.
3. Lower the heat. Cook until softened.
4. Add spinach, salt and lemon juice.
5. Increase the heat to medium/high. Sauté for a few minutes until the spinach is wilted.
6. Transfer the contents to a large ovenproof dish. Do not add the excess liquid that is present in the spinach mixture.
7. Make 6 wells or cavities in the mixture.
8. Gently break an egg into each of the wells.
9. Place the dish in a preheated oven. Bake at 300°F until the eggs are set.

10. Place a small saucepan over medium low heat. Add the remaining butter. When the butter melts, add the yogurt mixture and a pinch of salt. Cook for a few seconds and add oregano. Cook for 20-30 seconds and remove from heat. Discard the garlic halves.
11. Pour the yogurt mixture over the eggs and serve.

Cheese Muffins

Prep: 10 min	Total: 40min	Servings: 8

Ingredients:

- 1 cup almond flour
- 1/4 teaspoon baking soda
- A pinch salt
- 1/4 teaspoon dried thyme
- 1 egg, beaten
- 1/2 cup sour cream
- 1 tablespoon butter, melted
- 1/2 cup cheddar cheese, shredded
- 1/4 cup muenster cheese, shredded

Method:

1. Place cupcake papers in the muffin molds.

2. Mix together almond flour, salt, and baking soda in a bowl.
3. In a large bowl add butter, egg, and sour cream. Mix well. Add the almond flour mixture and mix well. If the batter is too thick add a little water or some more sour cream. Add cheese and mix well.
4. Pour into the muffin molds (fill up to 2/3).
5. Bake in a preheated oven to 350°F for about 20 minutes or until golden. A toothpick when inserted in the center should come out clean.
6. Remove from the oven and cool. Serve topped with butter.

Chocolate Smoothie

| Prep: 5 min | Total: 7min | Servings: 2 |

Ingredients:

- 2 cups, almond milk, unsweetened
- Few drops stevia of honey or agave nectar any other artificial sweetener to taste
- 1/2 cup heavy cream
- 3 scoops chocolate flavored whey powder

Method:

1. Place all the ingredients into a blender and blend until smooth and creamy.
2. Pour into tall glasses.
3. Serve immediately with crushed ice.

Green Smoothie

| Prep: 5 min | Total: 7 min | Servings: 2 |

Ingredients:

- 4 cups spinach
- 2 cups coconut milk, chilled, unsweetened
- 4 Brazil nuts
- 2/3 cup almonds
- 2 tablespoons psyllium husk
- 2 scoops whey protein powder
- 2 scoops greens powder
- 4 drops stevia or to taste (optional)

Method:

1. Place spinach, almonds, Brazil nuts and coconut milk into a blender and blend until smooth.
2. Add rest of the ingredients and blend until smooth and creamy.

3. Pour into tall glasses.
4. Serve immediately with crushed ice.

Berry Chocolate Shake

Prep: 5 min	Total: 7 min	Servings: 2

Ingredients:

- 2 cups almond milk
- 1/2 cup blueberries / blackberries / strawberries / raspberries
- 1/4 cup cocoa powder
- Stevia drops to taste
- 1/2 teaspoon xanthan gum
- 2 tablespoons MCT oil
- Few ice cubes

Method:

1. Blend together all the ingredients until smooth.
2. Pour into tall glasses and serve.

Matcha Smoothie Bowl

| Prep: 5 min | Total: 7 min | Servings: 2 |

Ingredients:

- 2 tablespoons goji berries
- 2 teaspoons matcha powder
- 2 tablespoons cacao nibs
- 2 tablespoons chia seeds
- 2 tablespoons coconut flakes
- 2 tablespoons chia seeds
- 2 cups coconut yogurt or full fat Greek yogurt
- 2 scoops greens powder (optional)

Method:

1. Add matcha powder, greens powder if using and yogurt to a blender and blend until smooth.
2. Pour into 2 individual bowls. Add the rest of the ingredients to the mixture.
3. Stir, chill for a while and serve.

Healthy Smoothie

Prep: 10 min	Total: 12 min	Servings: 4

Ingredients:

- 1 cup frozen strawberries
- 1 cup frozen raspberries
- 1 cup frozen blueberries
- 1 cup frozen blackberries
- 2 cups kale, stems and tough ribs removed, roughly chopped
- 2 cups spinach
- 1 cup orange segments
- 1 cup water
- 1/2 cup soft tofu

Method:

1. Place all the ingredients into a blender and blend until smooth and creamy.
2. Pour into tall glasses.
3. Serve

Ketogenic Soup Recipes

Chicken Enchilada Soup

| Prep: 15 min | Total: 45 min | Servings: 8 |

Ingredients:

- 2 tablespoons olive oil
- 6 stalks celery, chopped
- 2 medium red bell pepper, chopped
- 4 teaspoons garlic, minced
- 8 cups chicken broth
- 2 cups tomatoes, chopped
- 2 cups cream cheese
- 12 ounces' chicken, cooked, shredded
- 1 1/2 tablespoons ground cumin
- 2 teaspoons oregano
- 2 teaspoons chili powder
- 1 teaspoon cayenne pepper
- 1 cup cilantro, chopped
- Juice of a lime

Method:

1. Place a large pot over medium heat. Add oil. When the oil is heated, add celery and bell pepper. Sauté until the celery is softened.
2. Add tomatoes and sauté for a couple of minutes.
3. Add cumin, oregano, chili powder and cayenne pepper. Mix well.
4. Add chicken broth and cilantro. Bring to the boil.
5. Lower heat and simmer for about 20 minutes.
6. Add cream cheese. Mix well and bring to the boil. Simmer again for about 30 minutes.
7. Add lime juice, mix well and garnish with cilantro.
8. Ladle soup into individual soup bowls and serve hot.

Spanish Sardine and Tomato Soup

Prep: 10 min	Total: 30 min	Servings: 8

Ingredients:

- 9 ounces canned Spanish sardines in tomato sauce and olive oil
- 2 tablespoons olive oil

- 2 large tomatoes, sliced
- 4 cups fresh spinach
- 2 onions, sliced
- 2 cloves garlic, sliced
- 1 teaspoon black pepper powder
- 1 1/2 teaspoons salt or to taste
- 6 cups water

Method:

1. Place a large pot over medium heat. Add oil. When the oil is heated, add onions and garlic. Sauté until onions are softened.
2. Add tomatoes and sauté for a few minutes until tomatoes are soft.
3. Add sardines and sauté for a few minutes crushing the sardines simultaneously.
4. Add water and bring to the boil.
5. Lower heat and add spinach, salt and pepper. Let it simmer until spinach wilts.
6. Ladle soup into individual soup bowls and serve hot.

Hot Chili Soup

Prep: 10 min	Total: 45 min	Servings: 4

Ingredients:

- 12 ounces' chicken thighs
- 3 cups chicken broth
- 3 tablespoons olive oil
- 3 tablespoons butter
- 6 tablespoons tomato paste
- 3 cups water
- 2 teaspoons coriander seeds
- 3 chili peppers, sliced
- 1 teaspoon ground turmeric
- 1 large avocado, peeled, pitted, sliced
- 3 chili pepper sliced or to taste
- 1 teaspoon ground cumin
- 3 ounces Queso fresco cheese
- 3 tablespoons lime juice
- Salt to taste
- Pepper powder to taste

Method:

1. Place chicken in a skillet. Sprinkle salt and pepper over it. Pour about one tablespoon oil over it and coat well.
2. Place the skillet over medium heat. Cook until chicken is tender. Place chicken thighs into individual soup bowls.
3. Place skillet back on heat. Add remaining oil. When oil is heated, add coriander seeds and sauté for a few seconds until fragrant.
4. Add chili pepper and sauté for a few seconds. Add water and bring to the boil. Add salt, pepper, turmeric, and ground cumin.
5. Reduce heat and let it simmer. Add tomato paste and butter and continue simmering for another 10 minutes.
6. Pour soup over chicken.
7. Place a few slices of avocado in each bowl, a little Queso fresco cheese and cilantro and serve.

Chilled Avocado Soup

| Prep: 5 min | Total: 7 min | Servings: 6 |

Ingredients:

- 3 cups Hass avocado puree
- 3 cups vegetable broth
- 3 cups heavy cream
- 1/2 cup cilantro, chopped
- 2 jalapeno peppers, deseeded, chopped
- 2 teaspoons ground cumin
- 1 teaspoon salt or to taste

Method:

1. Add all the ingredients to a food processor and blend until smooth.
2. Chill until use.
3. Serve in individual bowls.

Light Zucchini Soup

| Prep: 5 min | Total: 25 min | Servings: 3 |

Ingredients:

- 1 medium zucchini, chopped into cubes
- 2 cups vegetable stock
- 1 small onion, chopped
- 1 small chili pepper, chopped
- Salt to taste
- Pepper
- 1/4 cup fresh dill, chopped
- 1 tablespoon olive oil

Method:

1. Place a pot over medium heat. Add oil. When the oil is heated, add onions and pepper. Sauté until onions are translucent.
2. Add stock, salt, and pepper. Simmer for 8-10 minutes. Add zucchini and simmer further until tender. Remove from heat.
3. Add dill and serve either hot or cold. For cold, chill in the refrigerator.

Cream of Broccoli Soup

| Prep: 15 min | Total: 30 min | Servings: 6 |

Ingredients:

- 1 large cauliflower, broken into florets
- 6 cups broccoli, finely chopped
- 2 yellow onions, sliced
- 2 teaspoons extra virgin olive oil
- 5 cups almond milk, unsweetened
- 1 1/2 teaspoons sea salt
- Freshly ground black pepper
- 2 tablespoons onion powder

Method:

1. Place a large saucepan over medium heat. Add oil. When oil is heated, add onions and sauté until translucent. Season with salt, pepper, cauliflower and milk. Stir and bring to the boil.
2. Lower heat and cover, and simmer until soft. Add half the broccoli and remove from heat. Cool for a while.
3. Add to a blender and blend until smooth. Transfer it back to the saucepan.

4. Add remaining half broccoli and onion powder and stir. Place the saucepan back on heat and simmer until broccoli is tender.

Cream of Mushroom Soup

Prep: 15 min	Total: 30 min	Servings: 6

Ingredients:

- 1 tablespoon butter
- 1/2 cup carrots, diced
- 1 onions thinly sliced
- 2 teaspoons garlic, minced
- 1/4 teaspoons dried thyme or oregano
- 1/4 teaspoon black pepper powder
- 3/4 pound white mushrooms, sliced
- 4 cups vegetable broth
- 1/2 cup water
- 1 cup almond milk
- 1 green onion, thinly sliced

Method:
1. Place a heavy saucepan over medium heat. Add butter. When butter melts, add onion and garlic and sauté for a couple of minutes. Add thyme and pepper, sauté until the onions are light brown.
2. Add mushrooms, sauté for a minute. Add broth, and water and boil.
3. Remove about 1/2 a cup of vegetables from the soup and keep aside.
4. Blend the remaining soup with a stick blender.
5. Pour the blended soup back to the saucepan. Return to heat. Add milk and the retained vegetables. Simmer for about 5 minutes or until thoroughly heated.
6. Garnish with sliced green onion and serve hot.

Ketogenic Salad Recipes

Tuna Salad

| Prep: 15 min | Total: 16 min | Servings: 2 |

Ingredients:

- 1 cup canned tuna
- 2 cups crunchy lettuce
- 1 hardboiled egg, chopped
- 1 spring onion, chopped
- 1 tablespoon lemon juice
- Pink Himalayan salt
- 1 tablespoon low-carb mayonnaise

Method:

1. Mix together all the ingredients in a bowl and toss well.
2. Serve.

Cold Chicken Salad

| Prep: 10 min | Total: 40 | Servings: 3-4 |

Ingredients:

- 6 chicken tenders
- 1 onion, chopped
- 4 radishes, halved
- 1 tablespoon fresh dill, chopped
- 1 stalk celery, chopped
- 1/2 cup mayonnaise
- 1 teaspoon salt
- 1 teaspoon pepper powder
- 1/4 cup minced dill pickle
- Cooking spray

Method:

1. Place the chicken in a greased baking dish and bake at 350°F until done.
2. Place radish in another baking dish and spray with cooking spray. Place in the oven and bake until done.
3. Remove from oven and cool. Chop radish into smaller pieces and place in a serving dish.
4. Add chicken and rest of the ingredients to it and toss well.

5. Chill for a while and serve.

Egg and Avocado Salad

Prep: 15 min	Total: 16 min	Servings: 6-8

Ingredients:

- 8 large eggs, hardboiled, quartered
- 2 large avocadoes, peeled, pitted, sliced
- 2 tablespoons extra virgin olive oil
- 8 cups mixed lettuce, rinsed
- 4 cloves garlic, crushed
- 1 cup full fat yogurt or 1/2 cup low-carb mayonnaise
- 2 teaspoons Dijon mustard
- 2 tablespoons fresh chives
- 2 tablespoons basil, chopped
- 2 tablespoons thyme, chopped
- Salt to taste
- Pepper powder to taste

Method:

1. To make dressing: Mix together yogurt, garlic, Dijon mustard and salt and pepper in a bowl.
2. Place salad greens and dressing in a serving bowl and mix well. Layer with avocadoes followed by eggs. Sprinkle salt and pepper and serve.

Tri Color Salad

Prep: 7 min	Total: 8 min	Servings: 6

Ingredients:

- 7-8 medium tomatoes, sliced
- 2 large avocadoes, seeded, peeled, sliced
- 10 olives, sliced
- 1 cup mozzarella, cubed
- 1/4 cup pesto
- 1/4 cup extra virgin olive oil
- Salt to taste
- Pepper powder to taste
- 2 tablespoons fresh basil, chopped

Method:

1. Add all the ingredients to a large bowl. Toss well and serve.

Caper and Lemon Salad

| Prep: 5 min | Total: 15 min | Servings: 8-10 |

Ingredients:

- 3 pounds' salmon fillet
- Salt to taste
- Pepper to taste
- Juice of a lemon or to taste
- 1 teaspoon lemon zest, grated
- 1/3 cup canned capers, drained, rinsed
- 3 stalks celery, chopped
- 3 teaspoons fresh dill, chopped
- 3 tablespoons extra virgin olive oil

Method:

1. Season the salmon with salt and pepper and bake in a preheated oven at 350 °F for 10 minutes or until the salmon is flaky. Let it cool for a while.

2. Transfer the salmon to a serving bowl. Add lemon juice and zest, capers, celery, dill and olive oil and toss well
3. Place in the refrigerator until use.

Salmon, Bacon and Kale Salad

Prep: 15 min	Total: 25 min	Servings: 6

Ingredients:

- 1 1/2 pounds' salmon fillets, skinless
- 2 bunches kale, discard hard ribs and stems, torn
- 8 slices bacon
- 1 cup almonds, sliced
- 1 medium red onion, thinly sliced
- 4 tablespoons lemon juice
- 1/2 cup olive oil
- Salt to taste
- Pepper powder to taste

Method:

1. Sprinkle salt and pepper over the salmon. Place the fillets into a broiler pan and place the pan in a preheated oven.

2. Bake at 425°F for 15 -18 minutes or until salmon flakes easily when pricked with a fork. Remove from oven and set aside for a while.
3. Meanwhile, place a skillet over medium heat. Add bacon and cook until crisp. Remove from pan. When cool enough to handle, crumble the bacon.
4. When salmon cools, break into flakes and add to a large serving dish. Add kale, bacon, onions and almonds. Toss well.
5. In a small bowl, whisk together oil and lemon juice. Pour over the salad, toss well and serve.

Thai Salad

Prep: 15 min	Total: 16 min	Servings: 3-4

Ingredients:

- 1/2 cup carrots, peeled, chopped
- 1/4 cup cilantro, chopped
- 1 clove garlic, minced
- Juice of 1/2 a lemon

- 1 1/2 cups kale, chopped
- 1 cup Napa cabbage, chopped
- 1/4 cup peanuts, roasted, unsalted
- 1 red bell pepper, chopped
- 1 cup thin coconut milk
- 2 tablespoons creamy peanut butter
- 1/2 teaspoon Sriracha sauce
- 1/2 teaspoon yellow curry powder
- Kosher salt to taste

Method:

1. Mix together all the ingredients in a large bowl and toss well.
2. Serve.

Ketogenic Main Course Recipes

Spicy Chicken Nuggets

Prep: 10 min	Total: 40 min	Servings: 4

Ingredients:

- 1-ounce pork rinds
- 16 ounces' chicken tenders, chopped into bite-sized pieces
- 2 tablespoons almond flour
- 1 egg, beaten
- 1/4 teaspoon chili powder
- Cayenne pepper to taste
- 1/4 teaspoon garlic powder
- 1/2 teaspoon onion powder
- 1/4 teaspoon Creole seasoning
- Salt to taste
- Pepper powder to taste

Method:

1. Blend together pork rind, onion and garlic powder, Creole seasoning, almond flour, salt,

pepper, chili powder and cayenne pepper in a blender. Transfer into a bowl.
2. First, dip a chicken nugget in egg and then in the almond flour mixture. Place onto a greased baking sheet. Repeat with the remaining nuggets.
3. Bake in a preheated oven at 400°F for 20 minutes or until brown and crisp.

Chicken in Butter Gravy

Prep: 10 min	Total: 45 min	Servings: 4

Ingredients:

- 1 1/2 pounds' chicken thighs with bones
- 1/2 cup water
- 1/2 cup pureed tomatoes
- 1/4 cup heavy cream
- 3 tablespoons butter
- 1/2 tablespoon olive oil
- 1 teaspoon coconut oil
- 3/4 teaspoon ginger paste
- 3/4 teaspoon garlic paste
- 1/2 teaspoon coriander, ground

- Salt to taste
- 1/2 teaspoon garam masala powder (Indian spice blend)
- 1/4 teaspoon Kashmiri chili powder
- 1/2 teaspoon paprika
- 1/2 teaspoon red chili powder
- Cilantro for garnishing, chopped
- Cauliflower rice to serve - refer to chapter 5

Method:

1. Rub the chicken thighs with olive oil, salt, and pepper. Keep aside for 15-20 minutes.
2. Roast in a preheated oven at 375°F for about 25 minutes or until almost cooked (it should not be fully cooked). When almost cooked, remove from the oven, cool. Remove the bones from the pieces and keep aside.
3. Place butter and coconut oil in a medium sized pan over medium heat.
4. When butter melts, add ginger and garlic paste. Sauté for a couple of minutes. Add tomatoes, coriander powder, chili powder, garam masala, paprika, and Kashmir chili powder. Simmer for a while until the butter is visible on top.

5. Add the chicken pieces, cream and water and simmer for another 5 minutes.
6. Serve hot garnished with cilantro leaves and cauliflower rice.

Ground Pork Tacos

Prep: 10 min	Total: 40 min	Servings: 8

Ingredients:

- 2 pounds' ground pork
- 1 1/2 teaspoons garlic powder
- 1 1/2 teaspoons onion powder
- 1 teaspoon sea salt
- 1 teaspoon ground cumin
- 1/2 teaspoon ground pepper or to taste
- 1/4 cup salsa
- 15 large lettuce leaves or more if required
- 3/4 cup green bell pepper, chopped
- 3/4 cup red bell pepper, chopped
- 2 medium onions, chopped

Method:

1. Add pork, garlic powder, onion powder, salt, cumin, and pepper to a skillet. Mix well using your hands.
2. Place the skillet over medium heat. Stir constantly and cook until the pork is browned well.
3. Remove the pork with a slotted spoon and place in a bowl. Discard the remaining fat.
4. Add salsa and mix well. Taste and adjust the seasonings if necessary.
5. Lay the lettuce leaves on your working area. Place some pork filling in the center.
6. Sprinkle peppers, and onions. Wrap it up and serve.

Italian Pork Cutlets

Prep: 10 min	Total: 45 min	Servings: 10

Ingredients:

- 10 pork cutlets
- 3/4 cup Italian dressing

- 1/4 cup parmesan cheese, grated
- Seasoning of your choice

Method:

1. Place the Italian dressing in a bowl. Add seasoning.
2. Place the cheese in another bowl.
3. Place a skillet over medium heat. Dip the cutlets in the Italian dressing.
4. Next roll it in the cheese and place in it the pan. Cook on both the sides until brown and cooked through.
5. Serve hot with Italian low-carb salsa.

Sri Lankan Fish Curry

Prep: 10 min	Total: 40 min	Servings: 6

Ingredients:

- 6 pieces (about 2 pounds) Silver Hake or any other white fish
- 6 tablespoons coconut oil
- 1/2 teaspoon whole mustard seeds

- 3 long green chilies, deseeded, cut in small pieces
- 1/2 tablespoon fresh ginger, grated
- 1/2 teaspoon ground cumin
- 1/2 tablespoon curry powder
- 2-inch fresh turmeric root, grated or 3/4 teaspoon ground turmeric powder
- 1 red onion, finely chopped
- 5 cloves of garlic, chopped
- 2 1/2 cups full-fat coconut cream
- 1 teaspoon sea salt
- Chopped cilantro to garnish
- 3/4 cup water

Method:

1. Place a large saucepan over medium heat. Add half the coconut oil. When the oil is melted, add mustard seeds. In a while it will start spluttering. When the sound of spluttering reduces, add onions and sauté for a few minutes.
2. Add ginger and garlic. Sauté for 4-5 minutes.
3. Add green chilies, curry powder, cumin powder and turmeric. Sauté for a couple of minutes more.
4. Add coconut milk and salt. Mix well and bring to the boil.
5. Reduce heat and simmer for about 15 minutes.

6. Meanwhile, add rest of the oil to a nonstick pan. Place the pan over medium heat.
7. Add fish to it and fry for 2 -3 minutes. When the underside is cooked, flip sides and cook the other side too.
8. Add fish to the simmering curry. Simmer for another 5-7 minutes.
9. Garnish with cilantro and serve.

Coconut and Shrimp Avocadoes

Prep: 10 min	Total: 20 min	Servings: 2

Ingredients:

- 1 avocado, peeled, pitted, chop into bite-sized cubes
- 2 cups shrimp
- 2 teaspoons Sriracha sauce or any other hot sauce
- 1 tablespoon natural peanut butter
- 2 teaspoons shredded coconut
- 2 tablespoons light coconut milk
- Cooking spray

Method:

1. Place a nonstick pan over medium heat. Spray with cooking spray.
2. Add coconut milk, peanut butter and hot sauce. Stir until well combined.
3. Add shrimp and cook until shrimp are tender.
4. Remove from heat and sprinkle coconut over it.
5. Place avocadoes on a serving plate. Place the shrimp over it and serve.

Baked Salmon

Prep: 5 min	Total: 1 hr. 50 min	Servings: 4

Ingredients:

- 4 salmon fillets (around 6 ounces each)
- 4 cloves garlic, minced
- 12 tablespoons light olive oil
- 2 teaspoons dried basil
- 1 teaspoon salt or to taste
- 1 teaspoon ground black pepper
- 2 tablespoons lemon juice
- 2 tablespoons fresh parsley, chopped

Method:

1. Mix together in a glass dish, garlic, oil, basil, salt, pepper, lemon juice, and parsley.
2. Add salmon and mix well. Place in the refrigerator to marinate for at least an hour. Turn around the salmon a couple of times in-between.
3. Transfer the salmon, along with marinade, to aluminum foil. Seal well. Place it in an ovenproof dish and bake for about 45 minutes in a preheated oven at 375°F.
4. Remove from the oven. When cool enough to handle, unwrap and serve with a low-carb salad of your choice.

Lamb Souvlaki (Greek Lamb Skewers)

Prep: 20 min	Total: 8 hrs. 45 min	Servings: 6-8

Ingredients:

- 2 1/2 pounds' lamb, chopped into medium size pieces
- 1/2 cup fresh mint, chopped or 2 teaspoons dried mint
- 3 tablespoons fresh rosemary, chopped or 2 teaspoons dried rosemary
- Juice of 2 lemons
- 3/4 cup extra virgin olive oil
- 1 teaspoon salt or to taste
- Melitzanosalata (eggplant dip) to serve

Method:

1. Add olive oil and lemon juice to a large bowl. Add salt, mint, and rosemary and mix well.
2. Add the lamb pieces and mix well. Marinate in the refrigerator overnight. Toss it a couple of times in between or more often.
3. Thread the meat pieces onto skewers. Place the skewers on the rack in a preheated oven.

4. Roast at 450°F until done. Turn the skewers around a couple of times in-between.
5. Remove from the oven. Let it cool for a couple of minutes. Remove from the skewers.
6. Serve with Melitzanosalata.

Ground Beef and Spinach Skillet

Prep: 15 min	Total: 45 min	Servings: 3-4

Ingredients:

- 4 tablespoons coconut oil or ghee
- 2 king oyster mushrooms, chopped
- 4 tablespoons raw almonds, chopped
- 3/4-pound lean ground beef
- 1/2 teaspoon chili pepper flakes
- A large pinch of Himalayan salt
- A large pinch of ground white pepper
- 1/2 cups pitted Kalamata olives
- 2 tablespoons capers
- 2 tablespoons natural roasted almond butter
- 3/4-pound baby spinach leaves, roughly chopped

Method:

1. Place a heavy-bottomed skillet over medium high heat. Add coconut oil. When oil melts, add mushrooms and sauté until brown.
2. Add almonds and sauté for a minute. Add beef, salt, white pepper powder, chili pepper flakes and cook until the meat is brown and cooked well.
3. Add olives, capers and almond butter. Mix well. Add spinach and sauté for a couple of minutes until the spinach wilts well.
4. Serve immediately.

Low-Carb Shepherd's Pie

Prep: 10 min	Total: 1 hr. 30 min	Servings: 6-8

Ingredients:

- 2 pounds extra lean ground beef
- 2 cloves garlic, minced
- 1 large yellow onion, chopped
- 1 packet frozen vegetables
- 4 cups cauliflower florets
- 2 teaspoons steak seasoning
- 2 teaspoons black pepper powder
- Sea salt to taste

- 1 cup beef broth
- 1 cup chicken broth
- 2 teaspoons dried rosemary

Method:

1. Place a large pot of water over medium heat and add about a teaspoon of salt and cauliflower florets to it. Cook until tender. Drain and set aside to allow it to cool.
2. Mash well and set aside.
3. Place a large skillet over medium heat. Add onion, garlic, and meat. Sauté.
4. Cook until the meat is browned and keep aside.
5. Remove the meat mixture with a slotted spoon. Drain off the excess fat and add the meat mixture back to the skillet.
6. Add steak seasoning, salt, pepper, beef broth, chicken broth and frozen vegetables.
7. Cook until the excess liquid dries up.
8. Transfer this mixture into a large baking dish.
9. Spread mashed cauliflower mixture over the meat mixture.
10. Place the baking dish into a preheated oven at 350°F and bake for 20 -30 minutes or longer if you want it browner.

Spinach Pie

Prep: 10 min	Total: 1 hr.	Servings: 4

Ingredients:

- 1/4 cup butter
- 1/4 cup chopped onions
- 2 packages (16 ounces each) frozen chopped spinach, thawed, drained, squeezed of extra moisture
- 6 eggs
- 3 cups heavy cream
- 1 teaspoon salt
- 1 teaspoon black pepper powder
- 1 teaspoon ground nutmeg
- 1 cup Swiss cheese, shredded

Method:

1. Place a large saucepan over medium heat. Add most of the butter. When butter melts, add onions and sauté until the onions are translucent.

2. Add spinach. Cook until the mixture is almost dry. Transfer into a greased pie pan. Sprinkle cheese. Place blobs of remaining butter in 4-5 places.
3. Bake in a preheated oven for about 30 minutes.

Low-Carb Pad Thai

Prep: 15 min	Total: 16	Servings: 3-4

Ingredients:

- 2 packets kelp noodles
- 1 large onion, chopped
- 6 cloves garlic, minced
- 1 cup peanut butter
- 1/2 cup soy sauce or tamari
- 3 teaspoons red pepper flakes or to taste
- 1/4 cup lime juice
- 1 large carrot, peeled, shredded
- 2 scallions, chopped
- 2 tablespoons fresh cilantro, chopped
- 2 tablespoons sesame seeds, toasted

Method:

1. Place kelp noodles in a bowl and pour water over it. Set aside for it to soak.
2. Meanwhile, blend together onion, garlic, peanut butter, soy sauce, pepper flakes and lime juice until smooth.
3. When the noodles have soaked, drain the excess water.
4. Pour sauce over it. Sprinkle carrots, scallions, and cilantro and sesame seeds over it and serve.

Stir Fried Bacon & Vegetables

Prep: 20 min	Total: 30 min	Servings: 3-4

Ingredients:

- 10 strips smoked bacon, chopped into fine pieces
- 2 cups kale, discard hard stems and ribs
- 1 medium head broccoli, chopped into florets
- 1 red bell pepper, sliced
- 1 cup green beans, chopped into 1 inch pieces
- 2 small courgettes, chopped
- 2 cloves garlic, chopped
- 2 teaspoons butter
- 2 teaspoons coconut oil

- Salt to taste
- Pepper powder to taste
- 1 cup thick single cream
- Cauliflower rice to serve – refer to chapter 5

Method:

1. Place a skillet over medium heat. Add coconut oil and butter. When it melts, add garlic and sauté until fragrant.
2. Add all the vegetables, salt and pepper and sauté until the vegetables are crisp and tender as well.
3. Add bacon and stir for a couple of minutes. Remove from heat. Add cream and mix.
4. Serve over cauliflower rice.

Zucchini Casserole

Prep: 15 min	Total: 45 min	Servings: 6-8

Ingredients:

- 12 cups zucchini, diced
- 1 red bell pepper chopped
- 1 yellow bell pepper, chopped
- 1 cup quinoa, cook according to the package instructions

- 1 1/2 cups cheddar cheese, shredded
- 3/4 cup olive oil
- 1 1/2 teaspoons dried basil
- 3 eggs, beaten
- Salt to taste
- Pepper powder to taste

Method:

1. Mix together all the ingredients in a bowl. Transfer to a greased baking dish.
2. Spread the mixture all over.
3. Bake in a preheated oven at 350°F until top is golden brown.

Low-Carb Pizza

Prep: 5 min	Total: 45 min	Servings: 6-8

Ingredients:

For pizza crust:
- 6 eggs
- 26 ounces' cream cheese, softened
- 1/3 cup parmesan cheese, grated

- 3 cups mozzarella cheese, shredded
- 1/2 cup heavy cream
- 1/2 teaspoon garlic powder
- 1 teaspoon pizza seasoning
- 2 teaspoons chives

For topping:
- 3/4 cup low-carb pizza sauce or as required
- Toppings of your choice (low-carb)
- 1 1/2 cups mozzarella cheese, shredded

Method:

1. To make crust: Add cream cheese and egg to a bowl and beat well. Add heavy cream, parmesan, chives, pizza seasoning and garlic.
2. Grease a baking dish and place mozzarella cheese into it. Pour cream cheese mixture over it.
3. Bake in a preheated oven at 375°F for about 30 minutes.
4. Remove from the oven. Spread pizza sauce over it and add toppings of your choice.

Ketogenic Side Dishes

Cauliflower Garlic Breadsticks

Prep: 15 min	Total: 50 min	Servings: 4-6

Ingredients:

- 4 cups cauliflower, grated, microwaved for 3 minutes
- 2 tablespoons butter
- 6 teaspoons minced garlic
- 1/2 teaspoon red pepper flakes
- 1 teaspoon Italian seasoning
- Kosher salt to taste
- 2 cups mozzarella cheese, shredded
- 2 eggs, beaten
- 2 tablespoons parmesan cheese powder

Method:

1. Place a pan over low heat. Add butter. When butter melts, add garlic flakes and red pepper flakes and cook for 2-3 minutes.
2. Add this to cooked cauliflower. Add salt and Italian seasoning. Mix well.

3. Add beaten eggs and mozzarella cheese. Mix well.
4. Transfer the mixture to a greased baking dish. Press well. Bake in a preheated oven at 350°F for 30 minutes.
5. Remove from oven. Sprinkle some more mozzarella and Parmesan cheese.
6. Bake for another 8-10 minutes.
7. Remove from oven. Cut into sticks.
8. Serve hot with low-sugar tomato sauce.

Keto Bread / Muffins

Prep: 5 min	Total: 35 min	Servings: 8-10

Ingredients:

- 6 large eggs
- 1 cup almond flour
- 3 teaspoons baking powder
- 4 tablespoons butter

Method:

1. Add all the ingredients into a bowl. Whisk well until the batter is smooth and well aerated.
2. Transfer to a greased baking loaf pan.
3. Bake in a preheated oven at 390°F for about 20 minutes or until done.
4. If you want to make muffins, then pour the batter into greased muffin tins (fill up to 2/3).
5. Slice and serve.

Mashed Cauliflower (Mock Mashed Potatoes)

Prep: 15 min	Total: 30 min	Servings: 6-8

Ingredients:

- 3 heads cauliflower, chopped into small florets
- 6 tablespoons heavy cream
- 3 tablespoons butter
- 3/4 cup cheddar cheese, shredded
- Salt to taste
- Pepper to taste

Method:

1. Place the cauliflower florets in a microwaveable bowl along with 1 tablespoon of cream and 1 tablespoon of butter.
2. Microwave on high for 6 minutes, uncovered. Add the remaining butter and cream.
3. Mix well and microwave on high for 6-7 minutes more.
4. Remove from microwave. Add cheese and blend with an immersion blender until smooth or blend in a food processor.
5. Add salt and pepper to taste.

Mushroom and Hemp Seeds Pilaf

Prep: 10 min	Total: 25 min	Servings: 6

Ingredients:

- 2 cups hemp seeds
- 1/4 cup butter
- 6-8 mushrooms, chopped into pieces
- 1/2 cup almonds, sliced
- 1 cup broth (vegetable or chicken)
- 1 teaspoon garlic powder
- 1/2 teaspoon dried parsley

- Salt to taste
- Pepper powder to taste

Method:

1. Place a pan over medium heat. Add butter. When the butter melts, add mushrooms and almonds. Sauté for a few minutes until the mushrooms are tender.
2. Add hemp seeds and mix well. Add broth, garlic powder, parsley, salt, and pepper. Mix well.
3. Lower the heat and simmer until the broth is absorbed
4. Serve with any curry or as it is.

Cauliflower Rice

Prep: 10 min	Total: 25 min	Servings: 4-6

Ingredients:

- 2 heads cauliflower, chopped into florets
- 1 onion, finely diced
- 4 tablespoons olive oil

- 4 cloves garlic, minced
- Salt to taste
- Pepper powder to taste

Method:

1. Add the cauliflower florets to the food processor and pulse until you get a rice like texture. You can also grate the cauliflower.
2. Place a large nonstick skillet over medium high heat. Add oil. When oil is heated, add onions and sauté until translucent. Add garlic and sauté until fragrant.
3. Add cauliflower rice and sauté for about 5-6 minutes. Remove from heat.
4. Sprinkle salt and pepper just before serving.

Ketogenic Snack Recipes

Healthy Granola Bars

| Prep: 3 min | Total: 20 min | Servings: 15-20 |

Ingredients:

- 3 cups macadamia nuts
- 3 cups almonds
- 3 cups sunflower seeds
- 3 cups unsweetened flaked coconut
- 3 eggs
- 3/4 cup coconut butter
- 3/4 cup organic peanut butter
- 1 1/2 cups dark chocolate chips
- 3 tablespoons vanilla extract
- 3 teaspoons pumpkin pie spice

Method:

1. Blend together all the ingredients in a blender until nutty or smooth. If you like them nutty, then make a coarse paste. If you like it smooth, then blend for longer.

2. Transfer to a greased ovenproof dish. Press well.
3. Bake in a preheated oven at 350°F for 15 minutes or golden brown.
4. Cool slightly. Slice into pieces and serve.

Fish Fingers

Prep: 15 min	Total: 35 min	Servings: 6-8

Ingredients:

- 2 pounds' fish like cod or snapper, rinsed, cut into fingers
- 4 eggs, beaten
- 1 cup shredded coconut
- Sea salt to taste
- 1 teaspoon garlic powder
- 1/2 teaspoon pepper powder to taste
- 1/2 cup coconut oil

Method:

1. Add coconut, salt, garlic powder and pepper powder to a bowl.

2. First dip the fingers in the egg and then roll in the coconut mixture and set aside on a plate.
3. Add 1/4-cup oil to a skillet and place the skillet over medium heat.
4. Add some of the fingers and cook until brown.
5. Repeat step 3 and 4 with the remaining fingers.
6. Serve with any dip of your choice.

Fried Cheese Sticks

Prep: 10 min	Total: 30 min	Servings: 15

Ingredients:

- 15 cheese sticks, frozen (do not thaw)
- 2 eggs, beaten
- 4 tablespoons almond flour
- 2 tablespoons ground flax seeds
- 2 ounces' parmesan, grated
- 1 teaspoon baking powder
- 2 tablespoons water
- Oil as required (coconut oil or olive oil)

Method:

1. Place a small, deep frying pan over medium heat. Add oil. It should cover at least 2 inches from the bottom of the pan. Heat until the temperature of oil is 375°F.
2. Meanwhile, mix together Parmesan, almond flour and baking powder in a bowl.
3. Add egg and water and beat well. Dip the frozen cheese sticks in this batter and immediately add to the hot oil. Cook until golden brown on all sides.
4. Remove with a slotted spoon and place onto paper towels.
5. Serve with a low-carb dip of your choice.

Pizza Bites

Prep: 15 min	Total: 35 min	Servings: 10-15

Ingredients:

For Pizza base:

- 3-ounce large pepperoni
- Pizza sauce, as much as required
- Grated cheese as required (optional)

For topping:
- Few olives, sliced
- 1 bell pepper, diced
- 3-4 mushrooms, chopped
- 1/2 cup green onions, chopped

Method:

1. Place the pepperoni slices on a lined baking sheet. Bake in a preheated oven at 400° F for about 7-8 minutes until the pepperoni is crisp.
2. Spread pizza sauce over each of the pepperoni. Sprinkle bell pepper, olives, mushrooms, green onions and cheese.
3. Bake for a few minutes until the cheese melts.

Ketogenic Dessert Recipes

Raspberry Chia Pudding

Prep: 5 min	Total: 19 min	Servings: 2

Ingredients:

- 1/2 cup vanilla flavored almond milk or soy milk, unsweetened
- 1/2 scoop vanilla protein powder
- 2 tablespoons raspberries, fresh or frozen
- 1 1/2 tablespoons chia seeds

Method:

1. Whisk together almond milk and protein powder.
2. Add chia seeds and mix well. Keep aside for 5-7 minutes. Stir again.
3. Repeat step 2.
4. Mix raspberries into it.
5. Keep aside for an hour in the refrigerator.

Berry Ice Cream

Prep: 10 min	Total: 4 hrs. 10 min	Servings: 6-8

Ingredients:

- 3 cups heavy whipping cream
- 1 1/2 cups blueberries or strawberries, or any other berries of your choice, unsweetened and extra for garnishing
- Few drops of stevia sweetener or any other sweetener of your choice (optional)

Method:

1. Add all the ingredients to a blender. Blend until smooth.
2. Freeze the ice cream for 5-6 hours or until set.
3. Remove from the freezer around 30 minutes before serving.
4. Garnish with the berries that you are using.

Strawberry Cheesecake

| Prep: 10 min | Total: 2 hrs. 15 min | Servings: 6-8 |

Ingredients:

- 1 cup cream cheese, softened
- 1/2 cup heavy cream
- 4 eggs
- 2 teaspoons lemon juice
- 1 teaspoon vanilla extract
- Sugar substitute like stevia, to taste
- 1 cup frozen strawberries, thawed
- 1/2 cup strawberry slices
- Whipped cream to serve

Method:

1. Place cream cheese, heavy cream, eggs, lemon juice, vanilla extract, stevia and frozen strawberries in a microwave safe bowl. Whisk well until smooth.
2. Microwave on high for 90 seconds stirring in between.
3. Cool and refrigerate.

4. Serve chilled with fresh strawberry slices and whipped cream or any low-carb sauce.

Chocolate and Peanut Butter Bites

Prep: 15 min	Total: 4 hrs. 15 min	Servings: 8-10

Ingredients:

- 4 large Hass avocadoes, peeled, pitted, chopped
- 1/2 cup peanut butter, unsweetened
- 1/2 cup cocoa powder
- 20 drops liquid stevia or to taste (optional)

Method:

1. Blend together all the ingredients, except peanut butter, until smooth and creamy.
2. Pour into a freezer-safe container. Add peanut butter. With a knife, swirl the peanut butter.
3. Freeze until done.
4. Remove from the freezer 15 minutes before serving.
5. Scoop and serve.

Conclusion

To conclude, a lot of the "low-carb" diets are being pushed around, but most of them do not succeed for one crucial reason: they do not include consumption of high amounts of fat in the diet! Without a high amount of fat in the diet, you end up putting on weight and becoming extremely lethargic.

This is because without both carbohydrates and fats in your diet, your body has no source of energy. So, your body starts conserving the little protein you consume, breaking down some of it to power some of the more important bodily functions, while saving the bulk of it for future use, making you extremely lethargic. This also means that whatever fat you do consume goes into storage, resulting in weight gain.

This is why the Ketogenic Diet has seen a higher success rate over the bulk of low-carb diets. A little planning and you will be well on your way to lose those extra pounds without putting in a lot of effort!

I would like to take the opportunity to once again thank you for purchasing this book and I hope that you found the content of this book helpful!

Stay healthy; stay happy!

www.ingramcontent.com/pod-product-compliance
Lightning Source LLC
Chambersburg PA
CBHW071026080526
44587CB00015B/2519